MAPPING EARTHFORMS

Mountains

REVISED AND UPDATED

Catherine Chambers
and Nicholas Lapthorn

Heinemann Library
Chicago, Illinois

Customer Service 888-454-2279
Visit our Web site at www.heinemannraintree.com

Designed by Richard Parker and Q2A solutions
Illustrations: Jeff Edwards
Picture Research: Hannah Taylor
Production: Duncan Gilbert

Originated by Chroma Graphics (Overseas) Pte. Ltd
Printed and Bound in China by Leo Paper Group

11 10 09 08 07
10 9 8 7 6 5 4 3 2 1

New edition ISBNs: 978-1-4034-9602-7 (hardcover)
               978-1-4034-9612-6 (paperback)

Library of Congress Cataloging-in-Publication Data

Chambers, Catherine, 1954-
  Mountains / Catherine Chambers and Nicholas Lapthorn. -- 2nd ed.
    p. cm. -- (Mapping earthforms)
  Includes bibliographical references and index.
  ISBN-13: 978-1-4034-9602-7 (library binding - hardcover)
  ISBN-10: 1-4034-9602-1 (library binding - hardcover)
  ISBN-13: 978-1-4034-9612-6 (pbk.)
  ISBN-10: 1-4034-9612-9 (pbk.)
  1. Mountains--Juvenile literature. 2. Mountains. I. Lapthorn, Nicholas. II. Title.
  GB512.C53 2007
  508.314'3--dc22
                    2006037718

Acknowledgments
The publishers would like to thank the following for permission to reproduce photographs: Bruce Coleman Ltd pp. **18**, **19** (J Grande); Corbis Sygma p. **26**; Corbis pp. **17** (Richard Cummins), **13** (Ron Watts), **25** (zefa/Guenter Rossenbach); Ecoscene p. **15** (A Brown); G R Roberts pp. **6**, **21**, **24**; Oxford Scientific pp. **23** (K Su), **27** (Mary Plage); Photolibrary/Pacific Stock p. **10**; Robert Harding Picture Library pp. **5**, **12**, **20**, **4** (H P Merten).

Cover photograph reproduced with permission of Corbis Royalty Free

Contents

Any words appearing in the text in bold, **like this**, are explained in the Glossary. You can find the answers to Map Active questions on page 29.

What Is a Mountain?

If you think of the highest places on Earth, where steep rock rises up into the clouds, what comes to mind are probably mountains. Mountains are huge, steep-sided rock formations that rise high above Earth's surface. Some people think that a true mountain on dry land has to rise at least 3,200 feet (1,000 meters) above sea level. Others believe that the exact height does not matter.

Mountains are often huddled together in large groups called **ranges**. There may be many mountains within a mountain range. Other mountains stand alone. Mountains can also be found under the seas and oceans, with just their tops sticking out above the waves. Other large mountains remain out of sight below the surface of the water.

▼ Uluru is a sandstone rock in central Australia. Uluru was formed when the softer rock around it was eroded. It is huge—2.2 miles (3.6 kilometers) long and 1.5 miles (2 kilometers) wide. It is only 1,100 feet (335 meters) high, so many people call it a rock, not a mountain. What do you think it is?

▲ Mountain ranges are often used as borders between countries. The Pyrenees mountain range, shown here, forms the border between France and Spain.

How are mountains formed?

Mountains form in three main ways. The first is when the giant **plates** of Earth's **crust** are pushed together or upward, and the surface rock crumples and folds. The second is when areas of soft rock are worn away, leaving harder rock sticking out high above the surrounding land. The third main way is when hot, soft rock from under Earth's crust shoots through gaps in the crust. It rises in a cone and cools into a volcanic mountain.

What do mountains look like?

Mountains give the world some of its most amazing scenery. The rocks make many different shapes, patterns, and colors. A very high mountain can be lush and green at its base but rocky and covered with snow at its **peak**. There are a large variety of mountain landscapes in the world.

Life on the mountains

There are many different types of soil and **climate** on the mountains. Life there can be tough, especially high up. Many plants have **adapted** to the cold wind and poor soil. Animals have learned to survive in the thin air and thick snow, and so have people.

The World's Mountains

Where in the world?

Mountains are found all over the world. Huge mountain ranges can cross **continents**. Occasionally, single **peaks** and **ridges** rise suddenly above flat ground. Some mountains are islands that pop up out of the sea. A lot of these are underwater volcanoes. They are found mainly in parts of the Pacific Ocean.

Most mountains rise in **ranges**. These are often found on the edges of the continents. Each range has a cluster of peaks, ridges, and **valleys** that all formed at the same time and in a similar way. Ranges are often separated by high, flat stretches of land called **plateaus**.

A group of ranges is called a mountain system or mountain chain. However, there are even bigger groups than this. They are known as **cordilleras** (belts). The biggest cordilleras on land are the Himalayas in central Asia, the Rockies in North America, and the Andes in South America. Even longer cordilleras can be found in the world's oceans.

▼ The Great Dividing Range stretches down the east of Australia. Rain falls on the east side as clouds are blown onto the land from the moist sea. To the west of the Great Dividing Range lies desert.

Mountains and climates

Mountains are found in all **climate** zones, from the frozen lands of Alaska to the hot deserts of the Sahara. The mountains themselves can have a big effect on weather. Mountain ranges make their own small climate zones. These affect the plants, animals, and people that live on the slopes.

Winds blow rain clouds onto continents. When the clouds meet mountain ranges, they quickly rise. The water in the clouds cools and falls as rain. The rain rarely reaches the other side of these continental mountain ranges. This is why so many deserts lie on one side of a mountain range. The deserts are in **rainshadow** areas.

▼ This map shows some of the major mountain ranges of the world. All of the mountains named in this book are also marked on this map.

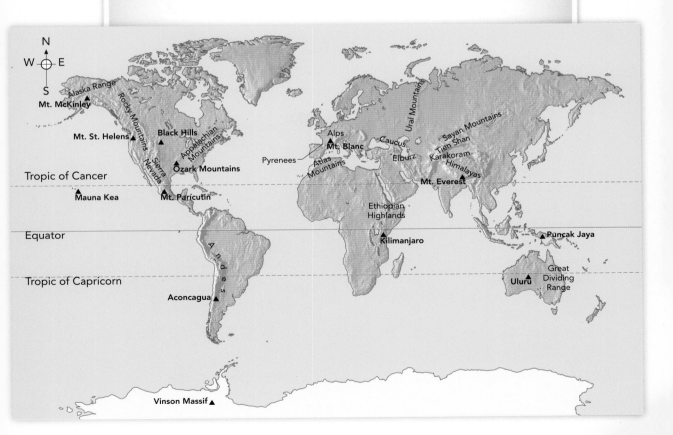

How Are Mountains Formed?

The moving Earth

Most mountains are formed because Earth moves. The **continents** rest on huge pieces of Earth's **crust** called **plates**. The plates move around on a layer of hot, **molten** rock. This layer is known as the **mantle**. Many of the world's mountains were formed millions of years ago when the plates bumped together and slid apart. Mountains are still slowly rising and changing shape as the plates continue to shift. This movement is called **continental drift**.

Fold mountains

In some areas, Earth's plates have been colliding together over millions of years and have pushed the crust upward. Huge mountain **ranges**, such as the Himalayas in Nepal and the Rockies in North America, have formed in these areas. Earth's plates are still moving slowly today, so these mountain ranges are still growing.

▼ This map shows Earth's moving plates. The arrows show the direction that the plates are moving in. They move up to four inches (ten centimeters) every year.

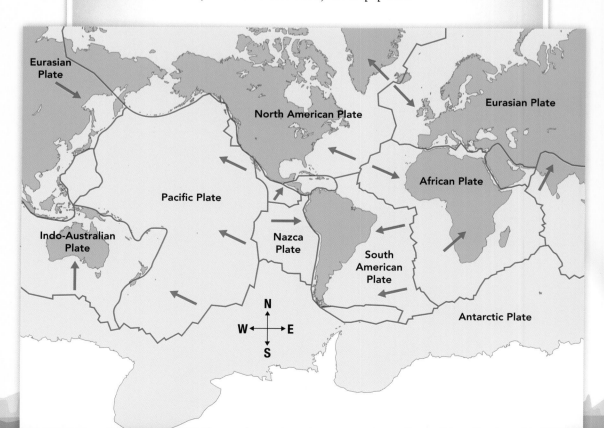

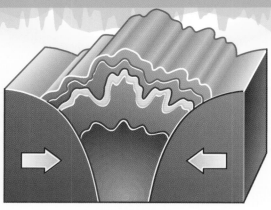
fold mountains

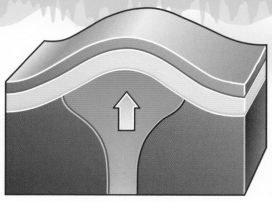
dome mountains

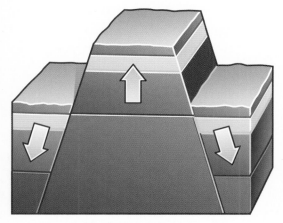
block mountains

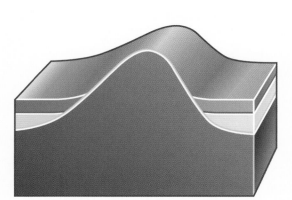
worn mountains

Block mountains

Movement under Earth's crust also makes cracks in the rock called **faults**. Blocks of rock slip up and down the faults. Some blocks rise above the others. These are known as block mountains. The Sierra Nevada range in the United States is an example of block mountains.

Dome mountains

Dome-shaped mountains were formed when Earth's movements pushed up hot, runny rock, called **magma**, from under the ground. The rock on Earth's surface was too tough to crack open, which left a dome shape. The Black Hills of South Dakota are dome mountains.

Worn mountains

Some mountains have formed where soft rock has been worn away by wind, rain, rivers, and **glaciers**. Areas of harder rock have not worn away as much. So the harder rock sticks high above the surrounding softer rock. The Ozark Mountains in the southern United States were formed in this way.

Exploding Mountains

Volcanoes

Volcanic mountains occur where the **magma** from below Earth's **crust** manages to break through and rise to the surface. Volcanoes can form where Earth's **plates** pull apart from each other. This creates a gap in the crust, and magma rises up through this gap. Volcanoes can also occur where plates collide together and magma escapes through cracks in the rock.

Volcanoes often begin with hot gases, ash, and rocks exploding out through the **vents** onto Earth's surface. Hot magma then rises up from huge chambers under the crust. When the magma reaches the surface, it cools and becomes **lava**, which is thicker than magma. Over time, many layers of lava may build up to form a cone-shaped volcano. At the top of the cone is the **crater** from which the lava flows. Sometimes lava is a bit thinner and runnier. It spreads out over a wider area, making a shield-shaped volcano with gently sloping sides.

▲ This lava is erupting out of Puu Oo vent on Kilauea volcano in Hawaii. The lava cools to form new rock on the mountainside.

Volcanoes can occur on land or under the ocean, where they often rise above the water as islands. The volcano Mauna Kea, on the main island of Hawaii in the Pacific Ocean, is taller than Mount Everest. It rises from the floor of the ocean, but only 13,796 feet (4,205 meters) of the mountain is above sea level.

Sleeping volcanoes

When a volcano has not erupted for millions of years, it is said to be **extinct**. However, a volcano that has not erupted for thousands of years is still thought to be alive. It is called **dormant**, which means that it is sleeping. Dormant volcanoes are very dangerous. Most of them have a **plug** of old, solid lava that fills the crater. When the volcano finally explodes again, enormous pressure builds up against the plug. This leads to a huge eruption. Mount St. Helens in Washington state lay dormant for 123 years. In 1980, however, magma pushed up against the solid rock, and the pressure blew out the side of the mountain.

▼ The diagrams show how the thickness of the lava affects the shape of the volcano. Thick lava cools very quickly and sets before it travels far, creating a steep-sided cone. Very runny lava will travel greater distances before solidifying. This type of lava forms a broad-based shield volcano.

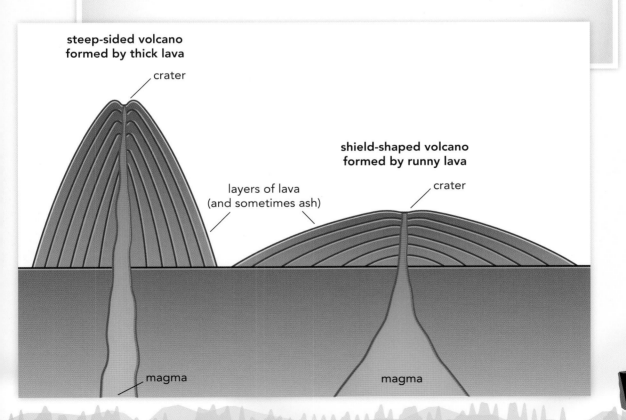

steep-sided volcano
formed by thick lava

crater

shield-shaped volcano
formed by runny lava

crater

layers of lava
(and sometimes ash)

magma

magma

What Do Mountains Look Like?

Mountains can have jagged **peaks**, rounded domes, or flat tops. They can be a single color or have bands of different colored rock. It all depends on the age of the mountain, the kind of rock it is made from, and the kind of **erosion** that has taken place. Young mountain ranges, such as the Alps in Europe, have tall peaks and deep **valleys**. This is because there has not been enough time for erosion to wear them down. Older mountains have rounder peaks and shallower valleys. The Appalachians in North America are like this.

Sun, rain, frost, and snow all wear down rocks. This is known as **weathering**. Wind, rivers, and **glaciers** carry away the pieces of broken rock. These pieces can scrape against the mountain and wear it away even more. The most powerful erosive force is a river. It can cut deep **gorges** between mountains. Frost shatters rocks into lots of jagged pieces called **scree**. These are pulled down the mountain by **gravity**.

▶ Erosion can reveal patterned layers of different types of rock, as shown in this image of the Grand Canyon. Different rock types are worn away at different rates.

Mountains are not just bare rock. Streams, waterfalls, and small rivers run down them. **Glaciers** slip slowly toward the bottom. Small lakes fill dips in the rock that were **scoured** out by the glaciers. Mountain peaks are often covered with snow, and snow sheets cover flat slopes. Lower down, plant life colors the mountain green except where the **climate** is very dry. Then, bare rock reaches right down to the valley floor.

Weather on the mountains

You can often see clouds, rain, and snow on mountains. Warm clouds blow against the mountain and rise up it. As the clouds rise, they cool in the chilly mountain air. This makes the **water vapor** in them turn into water droplets, which fall as rain or snow high up on the mountain. On the other side of the mountain, the cold air sinks quickly. This can cause very strong air currents.

▼ Mountain weather can change very quickly. It has a huge impact on mountain life.

A Great Mountain Range—The Rockies

The Rocky Mountains, also called the Rockies, are a long chain of mountain ranges stretching down the western side of North America. They first folded upward more than 190 million years ago. They are still forming and rising. The chain has many different landscapes, from the **peaks** of Wyoming to the flat-topped rocks of the Grand Canyon. Moving ice and water have caused most of the **erosion**. There are wide **valleys** that have been **scoured** out by **glaciers** and deep **gorges** carved by rivers. There are long ribbon-shaped lakes and hot volcanic springs.

The chain passes through many different **climates**, from the frozen lands of Alaska in the north to hot, sunny Mexico in the south. The Rockies also affect the climate to the west. They stop rain from reaching the west, making it into a dry **rainshadow** area. Many rivers begin high up in the Rockies.

MAP ACTIVE

*Describe the location of the Rockies, using the map. Mention the **continent**, the countries, the direction, and the position. Why do you think there are so many rivers to the east of the mountains?*

Life in the Rockies

Very small plants like **moss** and **lichen** grow on the upper slopes of the Rockies. Farther down there are grasses and small shrubs. Below this lie huge forests, mainly of **conifer** trees, with grassland sloping away from them. The vegetation makes a good **habitat** for many different **species** of plants and animals.

There are about five million people living in the Rockies. Many live in mining towns and cities. The mountains are rich in **minerals**, such as gold, silver, copper, coal, and iron ore. Natural gas and petroleum oil also are found there. Some people work in the forests, especially in the northern and Canadian Rockies. In the Colorado, Montana, and Wyoming Rockies, farmers raise large herds of cattle and sheep. Many people work in tourism.

◀ The Rocky Mountain National Park was created in 1915. It covers many mountain peaks, 60 of which are more than 11,482 feet (3,500 meters) high. Deer, Rocky Mountain Bighorn sheep, American elk, and coyote roam the park. Golden eagles circle overhead. There are more than 700 species of plants.

Mountain Plants

Growing problems

Different plants have **adapted** to different **habitats** on mountain slopes. On all mountains, plants face the same problems. Mountains can have changing **climate** zones as their height increases. As the slope rises, the temperature cools. For every 500 feet (150 meters) of **altitude**, the temperature drops by about 1°. Plants also have to cope with sudden temperature changes—from very cold at night to quite hot during the day. Mountain soils are thin and poor, and heavy rain high up makes any soil very wet. The soil often freezes, too. Strong winds blow around and down the mountainside.

Plants can grow higher up on mountains in warm areas of the world than in cold areas. In cold areas the temperatures are lower all the way up the mountain.

▼ This diagram shows how the plant life on mountain slopes is affected by the distance from the Equator. The snowline is the average height above which snow lies all year. The treeline is the average height above which trees stop growing.

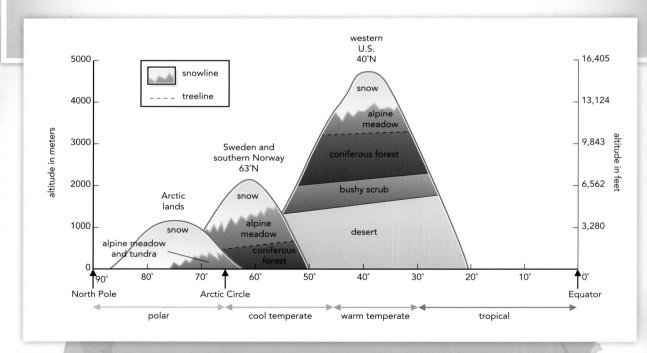

MAP ACTIVE

Describe the types of mountain vegetation nearest the Equator.

◄ Mosses and lichens cling to bare rock on the slopes of the Comeragh Mountains in Ireland. Because they are so low-lying, these plants are able to avoid the effects of the strong, cold winds. They grow very slowly, so people need to be careful when walking nearby in the mountains.

Tough plants

Plants have had to adapt to these harsh conditions. High up, tiny **lichens** cling to the bare rocks. They are very tough and do not need soil. **Mosses** are also tiny. They, too, can cling on and grow well in very damp conditions.

Lower down, larger plants often grow in sheltered cracks between the rocks where there is often a little soil. They flower and produce seeds in a very short time to avoid the long, harsh winters. Most mountain plants have very strong, clinging roots and short stems, which do not break in the wind. Their leaves are small, flat, and covered in hairs, spikes, or spines. These let in warmth and light but stop the wind and ice from harming the leaf. The flowers are surrounded by leaves for protection. Grasses have a tough, waxy coating and are often bunched together like a bush. They sway in a rotating motion so that they do not snap when the wind blows.

Mountains often have an area of **conifer** trees. Most conifer trees are evergreens, which means that they do not lose their leaves during winter. This enables them to use even winter's weak rays of sun to make food. The leaves are thin and often spiky, with a waxy coating. This stops them from drying out when the trees' roots are unable to suck up moisture from frozen soil.

Mountain Animals

Mountain animals have to survive in some fairly harsh conditions. There is less oxygen for animals to breathe high up in the mountains. This is because oxygen is a heavy gas that sinks. Many mountain **mammals** have developed large lungs and hearts to make the most of the small amount of oxygen available.

Many mammals live above the treeline. In the bitter winters, though, some move from the **peaks** down to the **foothills**. Small mammals, such as alpine marmots, eat as much as they can during the summer. They store fat in their bodies and then **hibernate** in winter. Not all mammals hibernate. Some have **adapted** to the cold temperatures. Large mammals, such as the yak, llama, and vicuna, often have long, thick fur. Their shaggy coats trap air next to their bodies, which heats the air and keeps them warm. The thick fur also protects them from the chill of the wind as well as from rain and snow.

▼ Mountain birds are usually large and strong like this golden eagle, which lives in parts of Europe and North America. It has to fly in very fierce winds. The female golden eagle is about three feet (one meter) long from its beak to its tail. Its wings are six feet (two meters) wide when they are spread out.

Mammals are often darkly colored so that they absorb the Sun's weak rays. Pale colors reflect more of the Sun's heat and make the animal colder. However, the Arctic hare and Arctic fox usually turn white in winter. This is because it gives them **camouflage** against the snow. It protects the hare from being caught by **predators**. It stops the Arctic fox from being seen by its prey.

▼ European brown bears live in the mountains. They often make their homes in caves. Their long, shaggy coats protect them from the cold, but in the coldest part of winter the bears hibernate. During hibernation, a bear's temperature cools and its heartbeat slows down. This stops the bear from using up energy stored in its body fat.

Mountain sheep, goats, and small mammals feed mostly on tough grasses and small shrubs. They can also eat **lichens** and **mosses** that cling to the rocks. The sheep and goats are able to climb on high, narrow ledges to find their food. The Rocky Mountain goat has soft hoof pads with hard, sharp edges. These allow it to run on hard rock or ice as well as on soft snow.

People of the Mountains

Why do people live on cold, windy mountains? Thousands of years ago mountain caves made excellent natural homes. They were easy to defend against enemies and wild animals. The mountains also provided wood and rock to build houses. Some people still make their homes in caves. Today, however, cave dwellings such as those in Andalusia in Spain have many modern facilities.

Many mountain homes have small windows that help keep out the cold. The roof slopes down over the sides of the houses. This catches the snow and stops it from piling up against the walls.

▲ Transportation and communication are very difficult in the mountains. Road and railway tunnels and bridges have been dug through the mountains to avoid the slopes. Cable cars carry people to higher parts of the mountains.

▲ New Zealand sheep graze high up in the mountains during the summer. In the autumn, as shown here, they are rounded up and taken down to the warmer **foothills** and flat **valleys**.

Food on the mountains

Sheep and goats can survive well in mountain areas. They provide people with meat, milk, wool, and leather. Farther down the slopes, farmers raise larger herds of sheep and cattle on the grassland. Fields of hay also grow there to feed the animals in the winter.

It is difficult to grow food crops on mountain slopes. Soil is often poor and gets washed away by the rain or blown away by the wind. Sometimes **gravity** slowly pulls the soil down the slope. This is known as soil creep. To prevent soil creep farmers build flat steps called **terraces**, with long walls to keep in the soil and water. Terraces are made in mountain communities all over the world, from Peru to China. Many kinds of crops, from rice to grapes, can be grown on terraces. Farmers grow an even greater variety of crops on the rich soils covering the slopes of volcanoes.

A Way of Life–Tibet

Tibet is an area of southwestern China that is enclosed by mountains on three sides. These include the Himalayas and the world's highest mountain, Everest. Most Tibetans live on a very high **plateau** between the Karakoram Mountains to the west and the Kunlun Shan range to the north. The average height of the land is about 15,000 feet (4,500 meters) above sea level. The region is known as the Roof of the World.

The Tibetan people have **adapted** to the cold temperatures and thin air, which has very little oxygen in it. They do not suffer from **altitude sickness**, a type of illness caused by a lack of oxygen in the blood. Tibetans have made good use of their harsh natural environment to make a living and build homes. The city of Lhasa is developing rapidly, and its population is increasing.

▼ The Tibetan plateau is ringed by many of the world's highest mountains. Many large rivers start high up in these mountains.

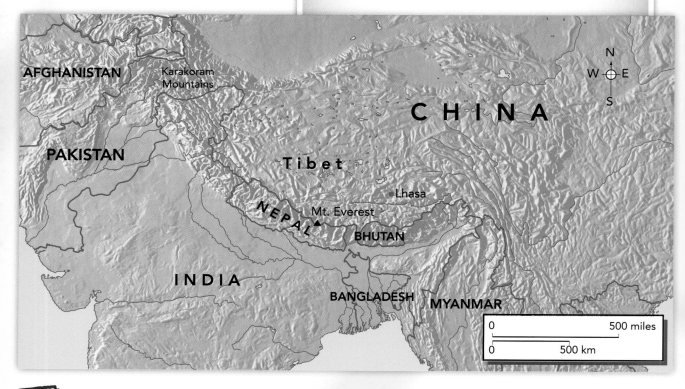

22

Making a living, building a home

Tibetan mountain homes are made from rock. They have thick walls and small windows to help keep out the cold. Some Tibetans are **nomads**. This means that they travel around with their herds of yaks, sheep, and goats to find the best pastures. They live in tents, often made of yak-hair felt, which they can easily move from place to place. They also keep cattle, horses, and shaggy-coated Bactrian camels.

▲ The yak is a very important animal for the Tibetans. They roast or dry yak meat to preserve it. They make the rich milk into butter, yogurt, cheese, and yak-butter tea. Yaks can be many colors. This is because they are often cross-bred (mixed) with cattle.

Mountain Tibetans grow barley, wheat, rye, fruit, vegetables, and root crops such as potatoes on their farms. Cooking is often done outside on a stove made of stone, with a wood fire underneath. Tsampa is a favorite dish, made of roasted barley seeds. The Tibetans make wheat flour into dumplings, which they stuff with meat. They make noodles out of flour. Some Tibetans make a living as mountain guides to foreign tourists and climbers. They also carry the climbers' equipment for them.

Our Changing Mountains

Natural changes

Mountains are changing naturally all the time. Earth's **plates** are always moving apart or pushing together, making the mountains rise. Mountain blocks push up or slip down along the **faults** that lie in Earth's **crust**. Hot **magma** continues to force its way to the surface, adding to existing volcanoes or making new ones.

Erosion is always taking place in mountainous areas. This makes mountains continually change shape. Sometimes huge boulders can break away and come crashing down the mountainsides. More often, the eroded material is made up of smaller stones and particles of soil, which get swept down to the **valley** floor. This **sediment** often gets carried away by rivers or **glaciers** sweeping through the valleys.

▼ You can see a lot of eroded material of all different sizes on this mountain. The small stones are called **scree**. This erosion has happened naturally over hundreds of years. It has changed the shape of the slope.

▼ Many important **minerals** and rocks can be found in mountainous areas. Humans have the technology to mine these out of the mountainsides. This leaves huge scars, such as those shown here at a marble quarry in Italy.

Human changes?

Mountain environments have changed a lot, especially in recent times. Mining has cut huge holes in some mountains. Many trees in the forests have also been cut down. This has left lots of mountainsides bare, and destroyed the **habitats** of birds, **mammals**, and other animals. The trees' roots no longer hold the soil together, so it slips and washes down the slope. Rain cannot sink into the soil. Instead, it flows over the bare rock and into the valley. This has led to more flooding in valleys.

There are also many more **avalanches** now. Trees help stop the snow from sliding down. But cutting them down can cause more avalanches. **Acid rain** has also killed trees in many mountain forests, which has added to the risk of avalanches. Some people think that avalanches are due to **global warming**. This is a change in Earth's **climate**. Earth is slowly warming, causing the snow to melt.

Looking to the Future

The process of mountains rising up and **eroding** will never end. The forces that make and shape mountains are mostly beyond our control. However, we can help look after the environment in the mountains and **valleys**. This will make them safe, healthy places for plants, animals, and humans.

Changes in the atmosphere

Global warming has been changing mountain **climates** and affecting mountain landscapes. What are the causes of global warming, and how can we stop it? Some scientists think that increased activity of the Sun is making Earth hotter. Others blame factories and car users for burning too many **fossil fuels**, which releases harmful gases into the air. They also believe that gases released by refrigerators and aerosol (pressurized spray) cans have destroyed the protective **ozone layer** around Earth, allowing more of the Sun's energy to pass through. Lowering the amount of harmful gases produced will help protect Earth's important ozone layer. It will also help reduce the problem of **acid rain**, which is destroying many mountain forests.

▶ Chamonix is a very popular ski resort in France. In February 1999 there were very heavy snowfalls and devastating avalanches. The worst avalanche hit buildings on the outskirts of the towns Le Tour and Montroc and killed twelve people.

▼ Empty oxygen bottles, cans, and plastic packaging litter climbers' base camps on Mount Everest. This kind of trash cannot dissolve and wash away. The problem of waste is growing on popular climbing **peaks** throughout the world.

Wearing away the mountains

The cutting down of trees has led to landslides, flooded valleys, and **avalanches**. One of the solutions is to cut down only mature trees and to replant new trees right away. People are now doing this in many parts of the world.

Tourists are another big problem for mountain environments. Hikers and climbers wear away plants and soil on popular mountain slopes. In parts of the United States, raised wooden walkways are used to protect the soil. More roads are also being built in the mountains to reach new tourist resorts. This leads to soil erosion and landslides. One solution might be to look at the mountains from lower down on the ground.

Mountain Facts

On top of the world

The Himalayas in central Asia have 20 of the highest **peaks** in the world. The next highest mountains are found in the belts stretching through North and South America. The list below shows the highest peaks on different **continents**.

Continent	Mountain (Range)	Height above sea level
Asia	Everest (Himalayas)	29,035 feet (8,850 meters)
South America	Aconcagua (Andes)	22,841 feet (6,962 meters)
North America	McKinley (Rockies)	20,321 feet (6,194 meters)
Africa	Kilimanjaro (Northern Highlands, Tanzania)	19,340 feet (5,895 meters)
Oceania	Puncak Jaya (Pegunungan Maoke, New Guinea)	16,499 feet (5,029 meters)
Antarctica	Vinson Massif (Ellsworth)	16,066 feet (4,897 meters)
Europe	Mont Blanc (Alps)	15,771 feet (4,807 meters)

- Did you know that satellite pictures are now used to measure the peaks of our tallest mountains? This makes the measurements more accurate. There have been many arguments about the height of Mount Everest!

Beneath the waves

- The longest mountain **range** under the oceans is the India and East Pacific Oceans **cordillera**. It is 12,000 miles (19,000 kilometers) long.

Not so steep

- The smallest hill in the world is marked on official maps of Brunei, in Asia. It is only 15 feet (4.5 meters) high and is part of a golf course!

Find Out More

Further reading

Barnes, Julia. *101 Facts About Mountains*. Milwaukee, WI: Gareth Stevens, 2003.

Morris, Neil. *Landscapes and People: Earth's Changing Mountains*. Chicago: Raintree, 2003.

Oxlade, Chris. *Earth Files: Mountains*. Chicago: Heinemann Library, 2002.

Web sites

www.mountain.org
Read about different mountain ranges all over the world. Learn how mountains form. Learn about mountain dangers.

www.nationalgeographic.com/ngkids/amfacts/snow_q1.html
Find out why snow stays on mountaintops.

www.nps.gov/romo/
Explore the beauty of the Rocky Mountain National Park.

Map Active answers

Page 14: The Rockies are in western North America. They run through Canada and the United States, all the way into Mexico. They run roughly north to south. Many of the United States' largest rivers flow from the eastern side of the Rockies. This is because most of the rain falls on the eastern side, as the mountains force the rain clouds high into the sky. This makes the clouds drop their rain.

Page 16: Closest to the Equator, the desert can extend quite high up the mountains, to a height of about 6,562 feet (2,000 meters). Above this is bushy scrub and then coniferous forest to about 9,843 feet (3,000 meters). Above this is alpine meadow and the snowline at around 13,123 feet (4,000 meters). Above this height is snow. All of these vegetation types can be found higher up than areas farther away from the Equator.

Glossary

acid rain rainwater that has been polluted by chemicals

adapted changed to suit certain conditions

altitude height of land above sea level

altitude sickness illness brought on by being very high above sea level

avalanche mass of snow that slides down a mountainside

camouflage color or pattern that makes an object blend in with its surroundings

climate rainfall, temperature, and wind that normally affect a large area over a period of time

conifer tree that has cones to protect its seeds and normally keeps its spiny leaves throughout the year

continent any one of the world's largest continuous land masses

continental drift movement together or apart of Earth's plates

cordillera large group of mountain ranges (also called a belt)

crater hole or hollow in the top of a volcano

crust hard outer layer of Earth

dormant volcano that has not erupted for a very long time but may erupt again

erosion wearing away of rocks and soil by wind, water, ice, or chemicals

extinct volcano that has not erupted for millions of years and is unlikely to erupt again

fault deep crack in Earth's crust

foothill any of the low hills around a mountain or mountain range

fossil fuel coal, oil, and gas formed from the remains of plants and animals that lived millions of years ago

glacier huge river of ice and compressed (packed) snow that slowly moves down a mountain

global warming gradual (slow) increase in temperature that affects the whole Earth

gorge narrow river valley with very steep sides

gravity force that pulls all objects toward Earth

habitat place where a plant or animal usually grows or lives

hibernate when an animal hides away and sleeps during the winter. Its heart rate slows right down so its body uses less energy.

lava hot molten rock that erupts out of a volcano

lichen not a true plant; a mixture of fungus and algae

magma hot molten rock that lies below the surface of Earth

mammal animal that feeds its young with its own milk

mantle layer of hot, molten rock that lies below Earth's crust

mineral substance that is formed naturally in rocks and earth, such as coal, tin, or salt

molten melted

moss small, green plant that grows in damp places

nomad person who moves from place to place to find food

ozone layer layer of gases high up in Earth's atmosphere that protects Earth from the Sun's harmful rays

peak highest point of a mountain

plate giant piece of Earth's crust that moves slowly over the mantle

plateau area of high, flat ground that often lies between mountains

plug solid, tube-shaped piece of volcanic rock that fills a volcano when it becomes dormant or extinct

predator animal that feeds on other animals

rainshadow area of low rainfall sheltered by hills or mountains

range group of mountains formed at the same time and in a similar way

ridge long, narrow peak, range, or watershed

scoured rubbed hard against something to wear it away

scree small, loose stones covering a mountain slope

sediment fine soil and gravel that is carried in water

species smallest grouping used to classify animals. The members of a species are very similar to one another and can mate to produce young.

terrace step of land cut into a hillside to provide flat land for farming

valley scooped-out, low-lying area of land between mountains

vent crack in the rock that magma can escape through

water vapor water that has been heated so much that it forms a gas that is held in the air

weathering action of weather on rock or other materials

Index